We Are Pitbulls

Portraits of the Dogs We Call "Pitbulls" and Their Owners

AnnaLisa Allegretti

Dog Park Publishing
Union City, NJ

This book is dedicated to all responsible dog owners, whether they have Pit Bulls, pitbulls, or money pits.

My heartfelt thanks to the participants of this project for their continued support through the many years it has taken to realize the end product.

For Laurelai

"Discover in all things that which shines and is beyond corruption."

- William Saroyan

WHAT IS THIS?

This is a book about differences, similarities and assumptions.

I started this project by asking people to bring their "Pit Bulls" and "Pit-mixes" to photo shoots in Pennsylvania, New Jersey and Maryland. I didn't ask for breeding papers, I didn't specify purebred American Pit Bull Terriers (APBT), I left it up to dog owners to identify their dogs as Pit Bulls or mixes, because they had decided themselves or been told by a shelter, a vet, or a DNA test that is what their dogs were.

The result is a collection of dogs that look very different from one another. The dogs featured here are Boxer mixes, American Bulldog mixes, Dogo Argentino mixes, Whippet Mixes and so many other kinds of breed mixes it will not do to list them all. Some of the dogs that look the most "Pit Bull" actually have the least APBT DNA according to their tests. My own Harrison is a strapping young fellow--robust, blocky-headed, strong, and someone cut his ears, but he is more Whippet than Pit Bull. Laurelai, the dog that started me down this road, appears to be purebred APBT.

The point is that while some of these dogs are purebred APBTs, the only true "Pit Bull," many of them look the part closely enough at first glance that they are lumped in to a loosely formed concept that is popularly referred to as the "pit bull" or "pitbull." For the rest of this book, I use the single word, non-capitalized "pitbull" to refer to dogs under this broad umbrella.

As you go through the book, you may say to yourself, "That's not a Pit Bull," and you may very well be right, but to someone--some landlord, some shelter volunteer, some Breed Specific Legislation enforcer, some fearful neighbor or police officer, that dog IS a pitbull, or pitbull-enough.

The misuse of the term is so rampant that "pitbull" has become nearly synonymous with "dog" and while it is true that today's All-American mutt has most of the characteristics that also define a true APBT, we are losing sight of what matters most: a good dog is a good dog, no matter what you call him.

The dogs in this book are each unique in their appearance and personalities, but they are united as good dogs, family dogs, therapy dogs, search and rescue dogs, and most importantly, happy dogs. They live with chickens, rabbits, horses, cats, other dogs, babies, cancer patients and humans with special needs.

The families in this book are part of a strong and growing movement of dog owners who advocate for education and understanding. These owners come from wildly different walks of life but follow the same road to liberate their happy dogs from the crushing weight of societal misconceptions. Hopefully, seeing how different each dog in this project is from the next will illuminate how impractical and absurd it is to refer to them all with one label of any kind.

So flip through and meet the dogs that we call "pitbulls."

LAURELAI, PERCY, & HARRISON

Laurelai, Percy and Harrison (not pictured below because I didn't own him yet!) work full time as office dogs in Philadelphia where they raise morale among their co-workers and amuse locals when they are all walked in together. These three have dealt with many fosters and are outstanding ambassadors to people and dogs alike. Their big brother is King, a 17h Thoroughbred gelding.

PERCY

LAURELAI

LAURELAI

Laurelai started it all for me. I rescued her from a backyard breeder in Philadelphia when she was six weeks old. This tiny brown mushball puppy inspired my parents to send me antagonistic news stories about "Pit Bull Attacks" and strangers stopped me when I was walking her to warn me that she would turn on me. Imagine how ridiculous that scenario looked when the wobbly brown thing on the other end of the leash wasn't even ten pounds. Just to be safe, I overdid it; I educated myself on the pros and cons of Pit Bulls, I had her formally trained as early as possible and completely made her a victim of "First Child Syndrome," which I experienced myself as the oldest of three. To her credit, she didn't let it get her down; she's a better dog than I could have ever hoped for and not because I made her that way. She can learn literally any trick, including opening the door, closing the door, jumping through and over obstacles, getting 'shot' and 'dying' dramatically, military crawling, standing up on her hind legs with perfect balance for extended periods, catching a biscuit off of her nose, holding objects perfectly balanced on her head, "placing" or sitting on desperately small surfaces like the cut stump of a tree, giving me 'five' (one paw) and then giving me 'ten' (both paws), answering the question 'do you want this?' with an affirmative bark, carrying anything you ask her to and finding specific toys upon request. I once used a dictation app to interpret her barking: the app registered her barks as "I love you."

If there's something she hasn't done yet, it's only because I haven't asked. At eight years old, she's still in her prime and we are about to start a nosework class together. Laurelai has grown up around horses, raised kittens, become besties with bunnies and pigs, and she absolutely insists that you love her, regardless of your species or natural proclivities. She has converted non-dog people to dog owners, non-pitbull people to pitbull owners, and more than once inspired the exclamation "That can't be a pitbull, she's so nice!"

But that's just it--she is so nice. She's so 'small' at 48 pounds, lightly built and athletic. She is a correctly built American Pit Bull Terrier and people are so often shocked because they expect an 80 pound slobbering behemoth. Laurelai adapts her play style so well to each dog she meets that it's practically a science. We call her the Mayor. She has ushered numerous fosters through our home and is the reason I now have two more dogs, both Pit Bull mixes. I think if she could do things over, she would reconsider being such an outstanding dog because then she wouldn't be living with so many other dogs on any given day. Most likely, though, she would do things just the same because she can't help herself.

Laurelai's favorite things, in order of importance, are: swimming, tennis balls, and food. If you offer her all three at once, she will choose swimming. In her case, 'swimming' means paddling obsessively in a circle, making huge splashes and biting them; it's not play--it is compulsion. She exits the water dangerously saturated if I don't force her out--red eyes, completely bloated and peeing every two minutes for the next six hours. Balls are next: tennis balls are preferred but bad for her teeth, so rubber balls are acceptable substitutes. Food... well... you can train this girl to do anything with food. She doesn't care a whit about keeping her girlish figure. Once, as a younger dog, while we were at a friend's establishment, she snuck off and vacuumed down an enormous bowl of kibble that did not belong to her. I happened to glance over just as she reached critical mass. A worried look crossed her face, a mix of confusion and discomfort, sprinkled with a desire to keep eating. She was about to blow. I picked her up and whisked her out of the carpeted room, but not fast enough; I was suddenly carrying a dog-shaped barfzooka as she horked up a perfect tube of glommed-together kibble.

Not the least remarkable thing about Laurelai is her enduring optimism. She had severe demodectic mange as puppy, with painful secondary infections and she was hairless for the entire third month of her life. She was comically unattractive during what should have been the most adorable phase of her youth, but her squinty wiggles still won people over. When she was only four years old, though she underwent three surgeries in one year (a major back surgery to repair a congenital defect and two ACL repairs), her spirit made it through intact. Today, newly eight years old, she runs and plays like she did when she was three. Laurelai is my once-in-a-lifetime dog. This project is for her and for all those dogs as wonderful to their people as she is to me.

PERCY

I wanted to rescue a senior dog, so I started looking and discovered the Urgent List from the Animal Care and Control of New York City. I called to rescue a senior pitbull named "Spanky" but I was moments too late. I was crushed, but the volunteer tentatively ventured that they had another senior dog they were having trouble placing, oh, and he would be put down the next day if I didn't take him.

Without knowing anything about this dog, I agreed to take him, figuring I'd find him another home if it didn't work out. Then she sent me a picture and I melted. I brought him home where he met Laurelai who had been waiting for hours while I was stuck in New York. She had to pee so badly she couldn't even take a moment to greet him, and he couldn't wait to sniff her, so she basically peed on his face. They've been best friends ever since.

Percy is incredibly obedient (when he hears you, of course). When I first brought him into the apartment, he walked into the bedroom, lifted his leg and started to pee. I said "NO" and he stopped mid-stream. He never did it again. He wanted to eat the cat, but I firmly discouraged that as well, and now the cat can rub himself all over Percy and Percy just wears his long-suffering expression of tolerance.

One of the most difficult dogs I've had, Percy had extreme clinical separation anxiety when I first got him. I had to medicate him to even begin behavioral modifications. Left alone for fifteen minutes in the kitchen once when I had to run out and fix a flat tire, he dug halfway through the solid wood kitchen door. There was blood all over from his frantic digging, heedless of torn paw pads and broken nails. Then he broke his tooth trying to get out of his crate. To this day, if I crate him, he works on a hole he has chewed in the plastic above the crate door to vent his frustration. He has long since been off of the medication and it has become apparent that his residual behaviors are actually due to the fact that he simply doesn't LIKE being left behind. He prefers to be in control of my coming and going and if I am gone too often or too long, he will find a way to act out. As recently as last year, his acting out involved sneaking into the kitchen and stealing a bunch of overripe bananas. I only realized what had happened when I saw an entire banana in the hallway leading to the bedroom; it had fallen off of the bunch as he carried them to his 'den' to consume them, peel and all.

My favorite Percy story comes from his first month with me. He is a Manhattan dog and as such doesn't have a familiarity with things like pools or accessible bodies of water in general. We were gathered at a friend's house, sitting on the patio with an in-ground pool between us and the backyard. Percy saw some dogs in the yard and wanted to go see them, so he shot off along the most direct route, which happened to pass over the pool. One minute he was running, the next he was gone. I leapt out of my chair, over the patio wall and to the pool where I pulled out a very surprised and deliriously happy-looking Percy--a look he gets when something he hates has just ended (i.e. nearly dying, being wet, getting his nails cut).

He was estimated to be seven or eight when I rescued him, and that was four years ago. He has barely aged a day, taking his second chance very seriously. His behavioral quirks have persisted as he's gotten older, but I love him all the same.

HARRISON

By the time I saw Harrison on the Urgent List at the same shelter where I had gotten Percy, I had fostered numerous dogs and had sworn I was taking a break. However, something about this dog, the way he sat in the courtyard at the shelter and quietly observed his surroundings, the way he looked up at the sky... I just couldn't imagine him on the pile of bodies he was destined for that day. It's rare enough that a dog looks up, but this dog looked up all the time, seeking freedom, understanding, something better. He had still-healing deep lacerations covering the top of his neck to the back of his head. We want to believe these were just embedded collar wounds from someone who left him alone as a rapidly growing young dog, but it's equally likely they are something more horrific. He has a collection of assorted deep scars scattered over his body--not consistent with anything in particular, though the marks across his forelegs and shoulders are consistent with a dog fight.

We will never know what happened to him. He's afraid of objects being held over him as though expecting to have them thrown at him or to be beaten with them. This normally exuberant dog cowers nervously when I sweep.

It almost seems as though whatever life he lived, he lived it devoid of human touch (except with objects of cruelty) and devoid of the sight and smell of the outside world, for he is forever just 'taking it all in.'

Harrison is the first foster failure I've ever had, but because he is such a 'tough' looking dog with such a vulnerable and sweet disposition I knew it would be a challenge to find a worthy owner. Beyond that, he had no canine social skills and had to learn them the hard way; by getting yelled at by lots of dogs.

He is also exceptionally strong and high-energy and even now, a year later, we are still working on channeling his energy and strength. Some of his expressions would be alarming to a normal owner--for instance, the noise he makes when he plays, a combination of lion and dragon with the crazy fierceness in his face, though it's all for show as he is careful not to put his mouth on you. I knew he needed to live with a dog trainer or an Olympic distance runner, and I was a little of both, so here he stayed.

Harrison is the perfect cuddler--he knows just how to share a space. He enjoys riding in the front seat of the car in his seat belt, sitting up like a person and attentively watching the world go by. Seeing him in the front seat brings a smile to most people's faces. He also likes to swim, and tries to play with Laurelai in the water, but she has no time for him because she is busy swimming in a circle and biting her splashes.

Harrison is named for Vonnegut's "Harrison Bergeron," the illegally strong, handsome and idealistic protagonist of the eponymous short story. Laurelai is my once-in-a-lifetime dog, but Harrison is my perfect match. He's still a work in progress, but he always makes me laugh. I am entirely incapable of getting mad at him because he does everything with such innocent glee.

CURI

Curi ('Curious') was adopted through a rescue group that found her at Animal Care and Control in Philadelphia. Curi is a very special girl; she helped her owners through the diagnosis of brain cancer in her Boxer brother, Chance, alerting them to when he was about to have a seizure. Curi then went on to obtain her Therapy Dog Certification and most recently underwent surgery for a cyst on her brain stem. Curi doesn't let that slow her down, though, as she keeps busy with agility and making sure everyone is smiling--especially her young human brother and her Boxer sister, Mya.

LUCY

Lucy came from the local shelter at the age of 6 months. Her adoptive mom was volunteering at the shelter at the time and brought her home as a foster, but of course, her foster family fell in love, and there she stayed. Lucy is a "Daddy's Girl" and loves people. She will go up to everyone she sees on her walks to say hello. Her favorite item of clothing is her tutu.

SODA POP

Soda Pop met his adoptive mom when he was 8 weeks and his former owner, a teenage girl, was told by her parents to get "that pitbull" out of their house immediately or they would take him to a shelter. Another foster failure and a true "Momma's Boy," Soda Pop is as sweet as his name implies.

SAVANNAH

Savannah came from an abusive home when she was 7 months old. She was terrified of almost everything but her adoptive mom. They built up her trust and she got much better but always carried a few fears from her past.

GIGI

Gigi was 6 months old when her owner brought her and her mother to the local shelter to be put to sleep, claiming they were tearing up his yard. Gigi was emaciated, with cuts covering her body and she had pneumonia. Today, she is a great little dog who is never without a chew toy in her mouth!

GRAYSON

Grayson was turned over from a cruelty case when he was 5 weeks old with two siblings, a brother and sister. Grayson is an old soul who just loves elderly people, so he visits nursing homes as a therapy dog.

EMMA

Emma was found in a school yard being teased by children when she was 3 months old. When her adoptive mom met her, Emma crawled into her lap and crossed her paws. It was love.

SIERRA

Sierra's adoptive mom went to an adoption event looking for a rescue to volunteer with and came home with Sierra.

RALLY

Just before Christmas, a severely emaciated momma dog was brought to the shelter with her newborn puppy by someone who claimed he had found them as strays. Rally was only five days old and not nursing; she and her mother were separated for foster care, but later reunited and their owners still keep in touch.

JETER

Jeter was found by his family through a rescue; he was brought in with his father and mother. His father has since joined Jeter's adoptive family after finding himself homeless again through no fault of his own. Jeter thinks it's pretty cool to have his dad around, now that he's not a teenager anymore.

NOLA

Nola is Grayson's (page 19) sister, though you could hardly tell to look at them. Nola is pint-sized and delicate where Grayson is sturdy and compact. Nola is a smart cookie, according to her people. She loves living with Jeter and his pops.

JETER

NOLA

KEVIN

Kevin, known formally as "Kevin Bacon," was taken in as a foster, but quickly became an indispensable part of the family. Kevin's favorite things are tennis balls, squeaky toys, grand adventures and spending quality time with his two human brothers, and of course his adoptive mom, who he adores most of all.

NALA

Nala's original owner got her as a 5 week old puppy, and decided after four months that he had had enough and was taking her to the shelter. Nala's adoptive mom took her instead. She was not looking for a dog at the time because she was going through chemo, but Nala provided the strength that her adoptive mom needed to get her through treatments.

KEVIN

NALA

GEISHA

Geisha was adopted from the local shelter where she had been turned in as an owner surrender by a mother who was tired of watching her son abuse his dog. Found by her current owner, a dog trainer, rescuer and breed advocate, she now shares a happy home with many other dogs, including her brother Xeric, an Australian Shepherd.

FINLEY

Adopted from Philadelphia Animal Care and Control, Finley has become his neighborhood's breed ambassador and resident greeter. Found wandering the Philadelphia streets with multiple bite wounds, Finley's gentle nature and exceptional handsomeness wins over everyone he meets.

BOOMER

Boomer was adopted from a local shelter, where he had been returned several times, for reasons unimaginable to his current owners and this photographer. Boomer is a perfect gentleman who simply enjoys eating, playing, taking walks, wearing a jaunty hat and most importantly, sleeping! Boomer gets to share the bed with his adoptive family and his canine brother, Mac.

BETTY

Betty's owner was convinced by her daughter of the virtues of pitbull type dogs. Mother and daughter started volunteering together at the local animal shelter in Trenton and began to bring pitbulls into their home as fosters. Upon arriving as volunteers to an adoption event, they were greeted by Betty--emaciated, missing patches of hair, but happy. Mom and daughter decided to foster Betty and fell in love. From a throwaway roaming the streets to a well-loved member of a multi-dog household, Betty loves to give her little "woo-woo" of happiness every day.

PENNY LANE

Penny is one of the dogs that Laurelai found a home for, in a way. Penny's adoptive dad knew Laurelai as a puppy and fell in love; he said he wanted a dog just like Laurelai, and that is what he got! Penny and Laurelai were twins when they were younger, but Penny has since far surpassed Laurelai in size. Penny's tail is always wagging and despite being such a large lady, she remains the little sweet puppy in personality.

CUDA

Cuda came from an accidental litter of rural pitbulls in Western Pennsylvania. He grew up to be a dashing 60 pound cuddlebug. When he isn't staring dramatically off into the distance or plotting his next squirrel-chasing adventure, Cuda likes to relax at home with his adoptive family. His favorite toys are laser pointers and socks. His best friend is a toddler.

DOMINOE

Originally hailing from Kentucky, Dominoe was rescued from a shelter in PA. He's a true momma's boy and loves to sleep like a person with his head on the pillow.

BAILEY

Found wandering in the woods in Virginia with a recently healed broken leg and 173 ticks for company, Bailey had been 'let go' by his original owner who was tracked down when he was found. She said that he had been hit by a car, so she didn't want him anymore.

DAKOTA

Dakota was listed on Craigslist at six weeks old because she was the last puppy, and black, so no one wanted her. She was going to be taken to the shelter, but fate intervened in the form of her forever home.

DRAKE

Drake hails from California, where someone found him in rough shape as an eight week old puppy living at the border of California and Mexico.

SAMPSON

Sampson is his adoptive dad's best friend. They have been together since Sam was six weeks old and are inseparable. Sampson's strength is in his hair, like his mythical namesake, so he is careful not to shed too much.

LUNA

Luna was adopted from a local shelter with two litter mates. Her favorite pastimes are eating, chasing the ball, swimming and sleeping under the covers.

SAMPSON   LUNA

CEDAR

Cedar was brought to New Jersey from a high-kill shelter in Georgia. His adoptive mom found him there and wasted no time in making him the light of her life. Cedar gets to enjoy many adventures, hikes in the woods, social events and he even models for a harness company.

COBE

Cobe was lucky enough to find the good life as a puppy and lives happily with his people in New Jersey. Cobe is a neighborhood celebrity, but he plays it cool with a very mellow demeanor and a casual toss of his perfect ears.

ENYA

Enya's owners have known her since the moment she was born, and she has cemented her place in the family by enthusiastically partaking in every activity, including hiking up big mountains. Enya loves to play at the dog park and loves everyone she meets.

GOTTI

Gotti's litter was motherless when the pups were just three weeks old, so his current owners nursed him into the robust and exuberantly friendly gentleman he is today. Gotti has worked extensively with focus training and even some interactive agility!

DIEZEL

Diezel is another strikingly handsome momma's boy. He and his human do everything together from car rides to hiking and swimming. Diezel loves adventures, spending as much time as possible outside and he is an excellent cuddler.

BELLA

Bella is a happy-go-lucky girl who is very loved by her family and friends in Baltimore. A dedicated sports fan, Bella does a "happy dance" every time the Ravens score a touchdown. Naturally, her favorite player is Torrey Smith and she hopes to meet his dogs someday to get their pawtograph.

ADDISON

Addison is a very intelligent and loved little girl with a ton of personality. Addison enjoys a good night out on the town, long walks on the beach, girl power and being adorable.

LUDO

Ludo was adopted by his family from a local rescue and quickly got used to having a giant yard, many doggy friends and countless tennis balls. Ludo spends his weekends adventuring in the countryside with his family and shares his home with a black rabbit named Lord Grantham.

ATHENA

Named for the goddess of wisdom, Athena likes to remind people never to judge a book by its cover. Rescued from a New Jersey shelter, she now spends her days in divine enjoyment, playing with toys, observing mere mortals and playing celestial games with her yellow lab brother, Zeus. Athena's favorite offerings are tennis balls, biscuits and cuddling.

LUNA

Luna found herself in a local shelter, where a rescue group snatched her up just in time. Sweet and energetic, Luna has participated in agility and search-and-rescue training to channel her energy. Luna's favorite activities are rolling over for belly rubs and giving kisses.

HUMPHREY BOGART

Known to his friends as "Bogey," Humphrey Bogart was found on the side of the road when he was about six months old. Luckily for Bogey, the folks that found him were active in rescue and took him in as a foster for a year before his forever family found him. Bogey is the in-house comedian and an excellent "small spoon." He has earned his Canine Good Citizen Certification and has helped his canine roommate learn how to forget her past and adjust to the good life.

BELLA

Bogey's people decided that they wanted their next dog to be a dog that needed more than the average amount of help; a dog that no one else wanted. A very pregnant and very scared female was turned in to the local Baltimore shelter. It took quite a bit of time and effort, but Bella was able to forget her past and look forward to her future with her lovely doe eyes.

BOLT

Bolt's original owner was arrested for homicide and Bolt found himself in a Baltimore rescue. Though he started out with ringworm, mange, and a serious eye injury from a dog bite, these days Bolt's defining characteristic is his calm and affectionate temperament. He gives back to his community by hosting foster dogs (over 10 at the time of publication) and currently lives in sunny California with his people and two pitbull sisters.

LUCY

Lucy's adoptive family had always had Golden Retrievers, but when they saw that Lucy needed a home, they set aside their apprehension about pitbulls (thanks in large part to Laurelai, the co-author of this project, and the one responsible for many changed minds and any typos) and took her in. Lucy is smart as a whip, petite and very affectionate.

BRODY

After Lucy, there was no turning back! Lucy's family met Brody at a horse show where a rescue had a booth set up. He was skinny and wiggly and wiggled right into their hearts, and Lucy's. Brody is a momma's boy and goes wherever his adoptive mom goes.

JIMMY   BRODY   LUCY   RILEY

BONHAM

Bonham's stunning good looks aren't all that make him special. Since being adopted, Bonham has used his irresistible personality and disarming handsomeness as an "on leash" control dog for a Baltimore dog training group and rehabilitation service. Bonham's favorite things are love, girls and other dogs.

SHEILA

Sheila is a little black bombshell with winning, squinty sweetness. Sheila is part of a growing household with many dog friends. Her adoptive dad keeps her busy with plenty of canine social activities.

CAROLINA

Carolina was rescued from a shelter in New Jersey and enjoys giving kisses and sitting on laps. Couches are also acceptable. Content to squeak a squeaky toy for hours on end, she passes the time contemplating the nature of squeaking and why the cats don't want to play with her.

CHAOS

Chaos' name seems tongue-in-cheek; he is dignified, observant and reserved. He exudes a peacefulness with a dash of enthusiasm for life and endless optimism. When he is not busy looking excellent in his Doggles, Chaos is a therapy dog.

CHOCOLATE

Chocolate was her family's first pit mix from a local shelter in Maryland. Chocolate likes playing fetch more than a little--she is completely obsessed with the ball. Chocolate inspired her family to foster other dogs just because she was that awesome.

TIM

Tim's family fosters for a rescue group in Baltimore. Tim came to them as a foster, underweight, ear infections and missing hunks of hair. Tim enchanted his people into keeping him and now he is part of a big, happy family dedicated to educating people about the true nature of pitbulls.

HARVEY

Harvey was found locked in the basement of an abandoned home. He arrived at the shelter almost completely shut down. He had clearly been left alone in the dark for some time; his collar was embedded, he had mange and fleas. His foster family brought the light back into his eyes and gave him a reason to trust people. Harvey was almost lost, but is one of the stories of a dog who has been truly saved. Harvey's foster family decided to keep him forever.

CHAUNCEY

Chauncey was rescued from a backyard breeder at the tender young age of six weeks. A dynamite and vibrantly enthusiastic personality, Chauncey inspired a passion in his adoptive family for the plight of pitbulls--they have since fostered over eight pitbulls in two years and are dedicated to promoting a positive image of these dogs.

LULU

Chauncey's family went to pick a friend for him from the shelter. He and Lulu hit it off right away and the entire family fell in love with her. Lulu's favorite things are Chauncey and tennis balls.

DEEBO

Deebo was living in a backyard as a six week old puppy until someone rescued him and he made his way to his forever home. He senses his adoptive mom's moods and health issues and is always there for her as a source of strength and reassurance.

DIAMOND

Diamond was rescued from the shelter the day after she was turned in; so many should be so lucky. She now passes her time as a girl's best friend and gets dressed up when she's feeling fancy.

KANGO

Kango is Chewy and Yodi's (page 95) father from an accidental litter of fourteen puppies! Kango was bounced around from home to home before finding forever with his current family. He loves to cuddle and share the couch. He is described as lovable, protective, funny and just a joy to have as a member of the family.

CHEWY

Chewy is one of the fourteen pups from that litter of love between Kango and his female friend Angel. He is described as a 60 pound lap dog. Chewy loves his stuffed animals and laying across the foot of the bed while his people sleep. Kango and Chewy live together happily and love to romp in the yard.

YODI

Yodi has been with his family since he was a tiny puppy. His personality is calm, relaxed and maybe just a tiny bit lazy. Yodi prefers to lounge around, receiving much-deserved affection. He is so well-mannered that people who typically don't like dogs will go out of their way to seek his attention.

PETEY

Petey was found as a puppy, tied to a fence in Philadelphia on of a sweltering July day, wearing a sign that said his owner could no longer care for him. His adoptive dad brought him in as a foster but fell in love with his energy and personality.

YODI   PETEY

YODI

CHEWY

KANGO

MAYA

Maya is another foster failure, rescued from a life of abandonment and seclusion in Baltimore, she now knows human love, kindness, and affection and gives it back exponentially.

DEUCE

Deuce was found wandering the streets of Baltimore, timid, hungry and alone, but he wanders no more and has furthered his family's passion for pitbull advocacy and education.

DESTINY

Destiny was moments away from euthanasia in a Georgia shelter when her humans pulled her through a local rescue group. She has received her Canine Good Citizen Certification, performed well in agility, has been in a magazine, and now, a book. Destiny celebrates her fame by giving hugs and kisses.

GYPSY

Gypsy was turned in to a humane society in Pennsylvania after being a breeding dog for a local fighting ring. She was emaciated and scarred. While Gypsy is still afraid of anything that is stick-like in shape, she loves all people and has learned to trust. She is still wary of other dogs, except for her Dogo Argentino sister, Lumen.

CHUNK

Chunk is a happy-go-lucky guy who was being fostered, but made himself indispensable with his "Welcome Home" dance. His adoptive mom realized she couldn't imagine coming home to a house that didn't have Chunk's unadulterated glee waiting for her when she opened the door, so she made him a permanent family member.

MOCHA

Rescued from a shelter in New Jersey, Mocha enjoys hugs, tennis balls, playing frisbee and supporting her friends in their battle against cancer by attending Bark for Life events. She lives happily with her English Bulldog sister, Penny.

DORA

Dora is deaf, but that doesn't stop her from adoring her people and being as sweet as can be. Dora helps her adoptive mom handle playtime with the kids and makes sure that there is an adequate amount of cuddling each day. When she's not too busy assisting with hopscotch, she makes good use of the clothes the kids have outgrown.

MOCHA

Mocha is the grande dame of her household and oversees all activity. She spends her days playing with children and helping her adoptive mom look out for other dogs who need rescue and help.

ROSIE

A Rosie by any other name would be as sweet. Rosie's adoptive mom was volunteering at a local shelter and fell in love with 9 week old Rosie who had a broken leg and was a bit cut up at the time. Rosie came home as a foster, but when an adoption fell through, her foster family knew it was because she was meant to live with them. Rosie shares her love and home with her canine sister, Ebony.

MILEY

Miley was adopted from a local shelter and enjoys standard doggy activities such as running, cavorting, gallivanting and sometimes just playing with her Shepherd/Greyhound mix sister, Zoe.

CHARLOTTE

Charlotte was confined to a basement for the first 10 months of her life, but now she much prefers sprinting across open spaces, exploring in the woods, playing with her other furry friends and running in circles to geometrically communicate precisely how many degrees of excited she is.

DYSON

Dyson is a sweet, happy boy who loves everyone and everything. He handles adversity with the greatest of ease and good humor. His personality and cheer are so outstanding that he remained super happy and greeted passing children even though his photo shoot was in the rain!

IZZY

Izzy arrived at a shelter in New Jersey as a dog-shaped mess of scabs, blood and red skin. Her adoptive family saw her the day she came in and fell in love with her, recalling how sweet she was through her discomfort. They applied for her that day, never heard back, and got a call nine days later to come get her or she would be euthanized--they came and got her right away. I had the distinct pleasure of hanging out with Izzy for a while so that her humans could see a local landmark and she is one of the very best canines I have had the pleasure of spending time with.

OLIVER

Oliver bears more of the traits of his mastiff side but has a little pitbull hiding in there somewhere! Figuratively, of course. Oliver came from an abusive situation but has won the adoptive home lottery and is learning to trust people more every day.

MAXINE

Maxine is a beautiful and talented Philadelphia native and has one of the most amazing pittie smiles. Maxine can do any trick you can think of, including standing on her hind legs in perfect balance.

CHLOE

Chloe's adoptive mom inherited her from an old
friend when Chloe was 2 years old. Chloe is known
for her cheerful greetings and wildly wagging tail.
Her favorite activity is burrowing deep under the
covers with another dog or even a human.

CHEWY

Three days before Christmas in 2009, Chewy wandered into a shop with no collar and no human accompaniment. No one seemed to be looking for him, so he went home with his new dad. Chewy likes to make a nest out of clothes when his family doesn't let him sleep in the bed.

MERLIN

Merlin was adopted from Philadelphia Animal Welfare Society when he was a year old. Merlin is an interesting mix with a disarming comic exterior, but he has plowed through his share of screen doors. He lives with happily with his adoptive mom and canine brother.

HOOCH

A happy and handsome pit mix, Hooch loves his adoptive human brother and the feeling is clearly mutual. Hooch relishes romping in the yard, playing with the ball and cuddling on the couch.

EMMA

Emma's family had been looking for a dog, and fell in love with her when they met her at a local rescue. They were surprised to learn that her DNA test indicated that she had Pit Bull in her, but are proud to love her and help her represent what good dogs Pit Bull mixes are.

LINUS

Linus was adopted from the local shelter as a companion for his owners' Boston Terrier, Sophie. Linus and Sophie hit it off immediately and love to sun together in the backyard or curl up inside with the family cat, Weston.

LORA

Lora was found on the streets of Philadelphia and taken in by a local rescue as the shelter had her listed for euthanasia. Her current adoptive family found her at the rescue and Lora struck gold. She now lives with a veterinarian in the beautiful suburbs of Philadelphia, doing whatever her people are doing--including runs, walks, hikes and attending local sporting events.

ROCKY

Someone abandoned Rocky in Trenton, NJ, at the local fire department, where he was taken to the shelter. With his time running out, his family found him and describes him as a bundle of mush. Rocky loves kids, cats and other dogs.

TYSON

Tyson is a purebred American Staffordshire Terrier. Tyson is sweet and gentle, and quite timid. He has a very charismatic and memorable personality neatly packaged into a compact and cuddly frame.

RUCKUS

Formerly living in a meth house, Ruckus now spends his time playing dress-up with the kids and sleeping under the covers. Ruckus takes his big brother duties very seriously for his canine and human siblings alike.

GHIA

Rescued on her way to the shelter, Ghia is a vibrant member of the family, following after her 'big brother' Ruckus in all things.

FRANKIE

Frankie was abandoned in an outdoor run at a shelter in New Jersey sometime on a chilly October night. His adoptive parents are volunteers at the shelter and fell in love when they met him, even though he was nearly hairless from severe demodectic mange. They fostered him for a month, and as so often happens, fell in love and adopted him. Frankie now visits elderly friends at a nursing home and hosts Pit Bull Awareness classes in Trenton. He has earned his Canine Good Citizen Certificate and is a therapy dog. He spends his days cuddling adorably with Lily.

LILY

Lily was another throwaway momma, found walking the train tracks in Woodbridge, NJ. The beginning of her life may have been rough, but she has long since forgotten, thanks to her humans, her brother Frankie, and the awesome house with a huge yard that her adoptive family bought just for her and Frankie.

MARSHALL

Marshall was left tied to a tree, like so many lost souls, but his family found him and showered him with love. He has a gentle, almost meditative demeanor and loves people, dogs and animals of all kinds.

LEO

Leo's mom is a veterinarian and he was brought in as an eight week old puppy after having been hit by a car. After rehabilitating him, she couldn't bear to part with Leo and brought him home. He goes to work with his mom nearly every day.

HELEN

Helen and her seven litter mates were part of a cruelty investigation and impound by Caroline County Humane Society in Maryland. Helen and her other six week old siblings were brought to the shelter with their mother and several other dogs. Mother and pups had been kept under the locked cap of a pickup truck on the ground and it was the middle of the summer. The property owner was charged with numerous counts of animal cruelty and served time. All of the puppies in the litter went to rescue or were adopted, except for Helen. Helen was profoundly deaf. One of the Humane Society's Board members took Helen home to foster her, and the family ended up adopting her. Helen is very attuned to body language and knows many hand signals.

LEVI

Levi was found standing in the middle of the road at the age of five months. Levi's owners never reclaimed him, so he went to live with Helen. Levi quickly became Helen's ears and Helen relies on Levi's cues. The two are inseparable and love sleeping nestled together on the sofa.

JUICE

Juice made his way to the shelter in Philadelphia after being taken to a veterinary hospital to have a bullet removed from his chest. His former owner was in jail for animal cruelty, and Juice has a wonderful life. He loves every human and animal that he meets.

LIBERTY

Libby was adopted from the Urgent List just in the nick of time at Philadelphia's Animal Care and Control. Libby is pretty sure she hit the jackpot living with a handsome hunk like Juice and her wonderful adoptive family.

JUICE

LIBERTY

VICTOR, MISS PIGGY, & LULU

These three rescued babies belong to a schoolteacher in New Jersey and LuLu comes to school as a Certified Therapy Dog to help teach children about looking for the truth beyond appearances. LuLu reads at a fifth grade level--an ability that comes in very handy at story time. Miss Piggy has been in a magazine, and now a book!

LULU   VICTOR   MISS PIGGY

MADI

Madi's adoptive parents went to the local shelter to look for a dog. Madi had just returned from a walk with a volunteer, and when they saw her, it was love at first sight. As first time dog owners, everyone learned together. Since Madi joined the household, her family has become more involved in community events and rescue, fostering many dogs in need and even adding another dog to the family. Madi has earned her Canine Good Citizen Certificate and brings joy wherever she goes.

MARLEY

When Marley's human saw his face staring at her from the New York Animal Care and Control Urgent List, she was living in a one bedroom condo and not looking for a dog, but she knew that she needed to save Marley. As his time ticked away, she had him pulled and two days later, he changed her life forever for the better. Marley and his adoptive mom now live in a house with a yard and couldn't be happier.

MOE

Moe and Midget make quite the pair! Moe is a gentle giant and loves his canine and human family. Moe is pretty sure that Midget is the big dog in the house and Midget hasn't corrected him yet.

MOIRA

Moira was being sold in an area where dog fighting is prolific, but her family got to her first and gave her a wonderful life. A unique and beautiful girl, Moira brought joy to her family, human and canine alike.

LADY

Lady crashed a Little League game but no one came to claim her. She scored a home run when her family found her at the shelter and brought her home. Lady's sweet smile and the twinkle in her eye are wonderful representations of her delightfully affectionate personality.

DUNCAN   LADY   MOIRA

SHADY JANE

Shady Jane was rescued at the age of six weeks from a backyard breeder, along with her sister, Nelou. Shady Jane is very attached to her sister and her owners, and won't stand idly by if they leave without her, often breaking out to find them.

NELOU

Nelou is a bit timid but not when it comes to seeking affection. She will stand on top of you until you make with the cuddles. Her new favorite pastime is kissing all the faces.

NELOU

SHADY JANE

NIKO

Niko is confident in his masculinity and still lets his mom dress him. He thinks that baby blue brings out his eyes. While he is obviously gorgeous, Niko doesn't let his looks go to his head. He enjoys the great outdoors and is exceptionally good at making people smile without even trying.

MYA

Mya was a stray on the streets of Baltimore, pulled from the shelter by a rescue group and adopted by her wonderful human. Mya keeps busy by improving the mood and lowering the blood pressure of the new friends that she makes on her adventures around town.

NYLA

At the time of the photoshoot, Nyla was an adoptable dog at the Caroline County Humane Society in Maryland. She was brought in as a stray. When her owners were located, they said they no longer wanted her and signed her over to the shelter. She loves people, other dogs and even cats. Nyla has since been adopted by a wonderful family.

CHANCE

Chance was found on the streets of New Jersey as an 8 month old pup. He was timid and shy, but has blossomed into a quietly affectionate companion. While he excels at agility and obedience classes, his favorite pastime is cuddling. Chance's owner never quite understood the affection people had for their dogs, but since she took a Chance, she totally gets it.

PEANUT

Peanut is presumed to be a canine-legume mix, but she acts more like a canine than a legume, most of the time. She was so malnourished when she was pulled from the shelter that she could not even walk. Now Peanut not only walks, but runs, rolls in deer poop, and supervises the host of other rescue dogs, chickens and children in her domain.

PEANUT

FLOWER

Flower is a treasured part of the family, keeping her humans and her human brother company. She loves to swim, retrieve, and look stunning in pictures. She may have learned the first two hobbies from her yellow lab brother.

GRACIE

Gracie is her adoptive mom's first foster dog. She had been brought to the local shelter with bite wounds covering her body. Holding no grudges, she gets along famously with dogs and kids and considers herself to be a lapdog.

HAZE

Haze was found in a bad neighborhood, tied to a fence with a shoelace, where he was passing his time playing nicely with a stray kitten. He was covered in bite wounds and had mange, but his forever family took him in, fixed him up, and never looked back!

ISABELLA

Izzie, as she is known to her friends, quickly made her way from the streets to the good life. She enjoys wearing her pearls, as they are functional and fashionable and is only too happy to tell you where "thump thump" is with a steady wagging of her tail.

JADA

Have you ever seen anything so beautiful? Jada was rescued as a puppy, born to a mother who was probably comprised of solid gold and rainbows, mated to a father who was diamonds and lighting. Jada is a stunner, and has a perfectly balanced, gentle, and beautiful personality to boot. She has no idea that she is a pitbull; she's far too busy being gorgeous.

LEXI

Lexi followed in the footsteps of many great pitbull-type dogs and was her family's introduction to pitbulls as well as a foster that insisted on staying permanently. Found on the streets of Baltimore at four months of age, Lexi had escaped a bad situation that left her fearful and dejected. When one of her humans was unpacking a new set of golf clubs the first week that Lexi was in the house, she ran upstairs and flattened herself under the bed. During Lexi's second week in the house, her people brought home a 12 week old puppy, her brother Jack, a Toy Manchester Terrier. Jack strolled up to Lexi and she began grooming and mothering him immediately. Today, Jack and Lexi provide the balancing influence each one needs, and Lexi spends her days changing minds for the better when she is out and about.

JERSEY

Jersey and her brother were left as four month old puppies in a box in the pouring rain overnight outside the local shelter in Florida. Jersey has repaid her adoptive family in spades for bringing her home, not least by saving her feline brother from getting lost. Jersey's humans didn't realize that the cat had gotten out, but Jersey did, and she held him gently until her family realized what happened and brought him back inside. The cat may not agree that he was "saved" in this scenario, but it was for his own good! Jersey loves children, other dogs, and sleeping under a blanket with her head on the pillow.

LACIE

Lacie is a beautiful princess who has enchanted humans her entire life. Since being saved from euthanasia as a puppy with her litter mates and mother, Lacie has inspired her adoptive family to educate people about the true nature of dogs like her, and has also convinced them to adopt a canine brother for her!

DELILAH

Delilah has inspired her adoptive parents to educate the public about what wonderful dogs pitbulls are. Delilah herself plays a very important role in this advocacy as she is the sole recipient of the plentiful pats on the head and scratches on the rump that are part and parcel of people changing their minds about pitbulls.

BODACIOUS, TOUCHÉ, & PATCHRONUS

These lovelies are purebred American Pit Bull Terriers and certified therapy dogs. Their human mom is very active in advocating for proper breed representation and sharing her pups' wonderful personalities with the world. These dogs are furry little superheroes, spending their days defying stereotypes and spreading cheer.

BODACIOUS

TOUCHÉ

ROMEO

True to his name, Romeo is a heartbreaker. This handsome boy loves to give kisses, even when there are far more exciting things happening on the beach. Romeo has a Juliet that he barks to each night, but he tries to keep that a secret from his adoptive parents.

RADAR

Radar was a little brown dog; she was found as a stray with an unknown history and found her way to one of the best homes in West Philadelphia, replete with giant yard, cat friend and bunny friend. Radar was a little old lady baby who was all at once an old soul and a mischievous youngster. She could totally work it when she wanted something from you. Radar developed a seizure disorder tied to a malignant growth, but we know that she lived a long, full life and had many adventures.

SCARLET

Scarlet enjoys chasing leaves and hopping from one end of the couch to the other to make sure that the furniture is balanced. She was a New Jersey shelter dog but is now a cherished family member, and maybe just a little spoiled.

AUDRE

Audre popped up on Petfinder when her humans entered "greyhound" in the search box. Audre has an extensive and diverse collection of balls, with which she enjoys playing fetch when she is not hiking in the park. She also likes giving kisses and hugs and being very much loved.

SANDY

Sandy, aka "Pickles," was found as a stray in New York, starving and still lactating from a litter of puppies whose fates are unknown. She has blossomed from a scared lost momma to a happy and social lady who is great with kids, cats, and dogs.

RUFUS

Rufus came from a pitbull rescue group finding homes for dogs out of a New Jersey shelter. He has completed his Canine Good Citizen Certification and visits Special Population children once a month at a local school. Rufus also participates in rally courses with his human and they are both very skilled at the sport.

BANE

Though he has not ravaged any cities lately, like his comic book namesake, Bane did grow up in his own version of prison. His original owner kept him confined and tied without food or water. He was dangerously malnourished when he was finally liberated. These days, Bane is an exuberant and energetic dog who knows many tricks and uses his powers only for good.

ROCKO

Rocko trotted through the shelter doors and straight up to his eventual adopter, who was there to pick up two dogs for a rescue, one of which he would foster. Rocko rode home with his head on his adoptive dad's shoulder and made his claim. Rocko had a rough start in life, being beaten and cut, but with his naturally sweet and optimistic temperament, you'd never even know. Thanks to his wonderful personality, Rocko is an excellent breed ambassador and has literally brought people together.

YODA

Yoda is a purebred American Pit Bull Terrier, and was the "runt" of his litter. Yoda is agile and delicate despite his robust physique and is very observant and engaging. It is a widely accepted fact that Yoda is the wisest and most handsome dog in the neighborhood. Yoda's favorite things are people and car rides.

STELLA

A lonely female pitbull was found making her way through the streets of Baltimore when a kind man took her in. To his surprise, she was pregnant and soon gave birth to 8 puppies. Stella's adoptive mom immediately agreed to take her and says she is her "heart dog" and that they are completely bonded. Stella's mom is now a board member of a pitbull advocacy group in Baltimore and a volunteer with the local shelter where more than a few pitbulls have found themselves. She says that Stella has changed her life for the better.

SONNY

Sonny was brought to a local shelter with his mother. Unfortunately, Sonny's mother was euthanized just two days before his adoptive dad met him. Sonny had won over the volunteers as he would easily win over his owner and everyone else that he met. About a year after getting adopted, Sonny's owner ran into someone who recognized Sonny and said that he was the only dog from the litter that the owner had kept and that he had been treated well until the owner got in trouble with the law. Sonny was diagnosed with cancer and cheerfully battled through chemo, radiation, surgery and finally the amputation of his leg. Sonny handled cancer and the loss of his leg the way he handles everything else; with a wagging tail.

PORSCHE

Porsche's owner found her wandering in the rain in Maryland. Perhaps she had been out looking for her new life, because she walked right up to her family and has been with them ever since.

TRINA

Inspired by the show "Pit Boss," a good Samaritan rescued Trina from a terrible living situation and brought her to her adoptive mom. She was only supposed to be a foster but... you know...

HARLEY

A thoughtful and reserved personality, Harley is a dedicated and loving member of his little family. Harley enjoys spending time with his canine brother, romping in the sand and studiously taking in the sights and sounds of the world around him.

NINA

Nina was one of my fosters; she was found running along the side of a major highway in Pennsylvania with her brother, Roo. Miraculously unharmed, they were picked up and brought to a local vet. When no one claimed them after a week, they went to foster homes. It became apparent that while they were in decent condition physically, they had been treated very unkindly; Nina was timid and fearful at first, expecting every motion to be a strike, but she came around quickly. She has a natural optimism and takes every new experience in stride. Roo had taken his past more to heart and it took him much longer to lose his serious expression and mistrust of people; but he absolutely melted when he met his adoptive dad and became an entirely new dog. A light came into his eyes and he finally seemed joyful. Nina now lives with a wonderful family with two children and a Chocolate Lab sister and I still get to dogsit her.

MISSY

Missy, another one of my fosters, was left tied to a pole with two other pitbull mixes in Brooklyn. She found herself at the shelter and quickly on the euthanasia list. Though she was spayed, microchipped and had had a bi-lateral femur repair at some point in the past, likely after being hit by a car, she was now dangerously malnourished, her teeth were caked with a quarter inch of black tartar and a pin from her femur repair was migrating out of her hip through a painful granuloma. Her white patches of fur were stained yellow--she had clearly been in a horrific situation for much of her young life. She was only about three years old when she came to us and according to her DNA test is actually 25% Wirehaired Pointing Griffon! Her optimism is relentless and she loves nothing better than playing and seeking affection. Missy is a perfect example of the positive canine spirit.

NAME UNKNOWN

This handsome boy is his adoptive dad's constant companion--accompanying him on errands, attending Relay for Life and Bark for Life events and just generally being helpful and showing off his excellent manners. His personality is very gentle and patient as he observes his surroundings and greets his many admirers.

ABOUT THE AUTHOR

AnnaLisa Allegretti lives in Philadelphia, PA, with her three dogs, cat, the occasional white rabbit, and horse. (The horse does not actually live in the apartment, as he found the stairs inconvenient.) Occasionally, there are as many as five dogs running about due to fostering and dog-sitting--it's a big apartment.

AnnaLisa became an advocate for pitbulls the moment Laurelai entered her life; such a wonderful dog deserved to be properly represented and understood. It quickly became apparent that Laurelai was the rule, rather than the exception--every pitbull that AnnaLisa has met in her years of veterinary office work, dog training and handling, behavioral evaluation, fostering and rescuing has been unfailingly sweet.

When she's not traveling the eastern seaboard to take pictures of pitbulls, AnnaLisa photographs horses, performs equine and canine massage as a certified therapist, paints pet portraits, creates 3D models and animations, and rock climbs. Her dogs accompany her nearly everywhere, including the office.

This is AnnaLisa's first published book. She hopes to continue the spirit of the project at www.wearepitbulls.com, gradually collecting more images of dogs labeled pitbulls.